tough times don't last, **TOUGH PEOPLE DO**

Copyright © 2020 Joshua D Ogunyemi

4Q Publishing Co.

All Rights Reserved.

All rights reserved. No part of this book maybe reproduced or transmitted in any form or by any means, electronic, or mechanical, including photocopying or recording, or by an information storage and retrieval system, without written permission by the author.

All translations of this work must be approved in writing by the author. Please contact 4Q Pro Financial for permission to translate and distribution agreements. Printed in the United States.

9 WAYS TO WEATHER THE STORM AND
COME OUT ON TOP!

tough times don't last
TOUGH PEOPLE DO

JOSHUA OGUNYEMI

What's Inside

Introduction
- About the Cover 3
- Tough times don't last, TOUGH PEOPLE DO 3
- Arks 4
- My Ark Experience 5

9 Habits of Tough People

#1 *TOUGH People [STAY]* Stick to It 9

#2 *TOUGH People [THINK]* Adopting a Positive Mindset 15

#3 *TOUGH People [TAP In]* Detours and Distractions 20

#4 *TOUGH People [Keep an OPEN Mind]* Be a Solution 26

#5 *TOUGH People [Create OPPORTUNITY]* Finding A Way ... 32

Creative Money Finding Methods

- **CMFM #1|** Unclaimed Money 33
- **CMFM #2|** Attracting Money 37
- **CMFM|** Brainstorm 38
- **CMFM #3|** OPM (Other People's Money) 39
- **CMFM #4|** Shop Your House 39
- **CMFM #5|** Survey Says 39
- **CMFM #6|** Cut Your Cable 40
- **CMFM #7|** Use Your Car 40
- **CMFM #8|** Collaboration Over Competition 41

#6 *TOUGH People [OWN IT]* Own Your I.P. 43

#7 *TOUGH People [UNDERSTAND]* Reflecting on the Past ... 45

#8 *TOUGH People [GROW]* Uncomfortable Spaces 47

#9 *TOUGH People [HELP]* Not in Vain 50

Introduction
About the Cover

There's a familiar story *I'm sure you've heard it* known as "Noah's Ark." It is centered on Noah's experience during the time of the Great Flood-- *a storm said to have destroyed the world leaving only Noah and his wife, his three sons, and their wives.*

As the story goes, Noah and his family survived the storm aboard a massive wooden ship that Noah had built. It was called an ark. This book is inspired by Noah's experience during a "tough" time in his life. I'll reference his story as a blueprint for getting through challenging times.

tough times don't last TOUGH People DO

This is a common phrase and mostly self-explanatory: tough times are temporary while **TOUGH** people stand the tests of time. On another note, this book is geared toward taking **ACTION**. As you read you will identify important habits to help you win during tough times...things **TOUGH** People DO.

Arks

Noah anticipated the storm by building a vessel that would isolate him with his family to shield them from the most devastating effects of the storm *sounds familiar!* Noah's ark kept them afloat during a very turbulent time

...long enough for the storm blow over.

Looking back over my life and thinking things over, I've been through some challenging situations. I can truly say, though, that I've been *so* blessed! Looking back through the storms I've faced, I can see where there was always an ark.

There was always "something" keeping my faith, covering my family, and protecting my sanity.

I've failed many times, *including losing multiple jobs*. I could have lost hope or walked out on my family. *BUT* no matter how bad things have gotten, we SURVIVED.

<u>You</u> *survived.*

Somehow, we managed to keep our heads above water until the storm blew over. Not only that, but we also came out of the storm *each time* on a new level—**stronger, wiser, better!**

...Let's connect the dots....
My Ark Experience

In January 2013, just two days after our wedding, *the "calm,"* my wife, Michelle went into labor with our twin girls at **23 WEEKS**

about four months premature.

The "Storm"

The doctors conducted emergency surgery and delivered our babies, each weighed **1 pound 3 ounces**. They were the size of Barbie dolls. Right away, the girls went silently out of the operating room straight to intensive care. Just **1 day later**, we said goodbye to our daughter, Morgan while Kennedy **fought for her life**.

We couldn't hold her for a long time. Her body was *so* fragile. The risk for injury and infection was high. And her skin was *less than* paper thin. Her body was so underdeveloped at birth, that she spent the next **6 months** inside an incubator. The incubator was crucial for Kennedy, and an ideal situation for her development *given the circumstances*. It gave her just the right amount of oxygen, heat, humidity, and light. The incubator kept Kennedy protected and kept her afloat while her vital organs developed. That was Kennedy's ark. We got to see firsthand the growth and developments that a baby would *normally* experience inside her mother.

Meanwhile, *without us really knowing it*, as Kennedy developed physically, Michelle & I developed spiritually, mentally, emotionally. It was one of the most challenging times of *my* life, certainly our life together but it caused our marriage to develop. It tested us in *every* way imaginable and we were made better for it. I got a crash course on being a husband, how to pray for *and* with my wife. I learned how to be strong for my family. It pushed me to

tough times don't last, **TOUGH PEOPLE DO**

be a dependable father

stand on God's word

stay strong in faith

be resilient

be patient

be TOUGH and stick it out!

...in conclusion

The ark is a sign of development *like an incubator or cocoon*. It's a built environment that fosters your development.

> I want YOU to look back. As you read this book, take some time to reflect on
> **areas where you've grown**
>
> **strengths you've developed** and
>
> **ways you've improved**.

As you identify YOUR arks, you will see challenging times as **necessary** to your development and learn to appreciate the storms.

Coming attractions...

This part isn't spelled out for us in the story, but I *can* imagine what life must have been like for Noah aboard his ark in the middle of the storm. *It sounds a lot like our lives today!* In this book we'll cover topics like:

> **How to Navigate the Day-To-Day Stressors**
>
> **Detours and Distractions** and
>
> **How to Grow Through Tough Times**.

tough times don't last, **TOUGH PEOPLE DO**

Don't worry. This won't be another boring book. This one is different. I wrote it with you in mind—to help you with your life, your problems. You'll find valuable quotes, affirmations and tasks for practical application. In case you're not a big reader, or a little short on time, here is a one sentence summary of the entire book:

There are a few key habits you can commit to TODAY that will help
YOU WIN
in challenging times.

TOUGH People
[STAY]

Stick to It

#1 TOUGH People [STAY] *Stick to It*

Times are as tough as they have ever been, and we have so many challenges to navigate. I remember some of the most challenging storms I've experienced *like you, I've seen a thing or two* and I noticed a particular pattern in the way I responded in tough times. Any time the "stuff" hit the fan and times have gotten tough, I've learned to just wait

...with **deliberate patience**, just wait.

It's like my superpower— *MY "STICK-TO-IT-NESS."*— only in the sense that it comes naturally. I've been this way since birth *ask my mom... she was in labor with me for a week!*

But
Patience doesn't come easy. It requires work!

"When the going gets tough,
~~the tough get going.~~"
I AIN'T GOIN' NOWHERE

tough times don't last, **TOUGH PEOPLE DO**

TOUGH People [STAY] *Stick to It*

If you've contemplated giving up, you're on the brink of a nervous breakdown, OR maybe you've decided divorce is the only option,

STAY.

I know it's an uncomfortable situation. I know you feel frustrated. I know there's a ton of pressure and it feels like the weight of the world is on your shoulders.

STAY.

How do you keep your marriage together? How can you turn your situation around?

STAY.

You get the idea by now. I know this is the Introduction, here's a bonus before you get started. **TOUGH People STAY!**

If you can keep your head when all about you
Are losing theirs and blaming it on you,
If you can trust yourself when all men doubt you,
But make for their doubting too;
If you can wait and not be tired by waiting,
Or, being lied about, don't deal in lies,
Or, being hated, don't give way to hating,
And yet don't look too good, nor talk too wise:

If you can dream – and not make dreams your master;
If you can think – and not make thoughts your aim;
If you can meet with Triumph and Disaster
And treat those two impostors the same;
If you can bear to hear the truth you've spoken
Twisted by knaves to make a trap for fools,
Or watch the things you gave your life to, broken,
And stoop and build 'em up with worn-out tools;

If you can make one heap of all your winnings
And risk it on one turn of pitch-and-toss,
And lose, and start again at your beginnings
And never breathe a word about your loss;
If you can force your heart and nerve and sinew
To serve your turn long after they are gone,
And so hold on when there is nothing in you
Except the Will which says to them: 'Hold on!'

If you can talk with crowds and keep your virtue,
Or walk with Kings – nor lose the common touch,
If neither foes nor loving friends can hurt you,
If all men count with you, but none too much;
If you can fill the unforgiving minute
With sixty seconds' worth of distance run,
Yours is the Earth and everything that's in it,
And – which is more – you'll be a Man, my son!

"If" by Rudyard Kipling

There are a few key habits you can commit to <u>TODAY</u> that will help
YOU WIN
in challenging times

Full disclosure: I still have moments when frustration and anxiety are **through the roof** just like everybody else. I have learned a lot in managing the ups and downs, how to

bounce back and keep on going.

With all the challenges we face today, it's normal to feel a little stressed. Dealing with the effects of the pandemic, the social tension, racial injustice, problems with the election and corrupt-as-ever politics, **on top of** whatever personal issues we're facing, a lot of people are stressed out!

These are tough times to deal with and I thought you could use a guide, something to encourage *and equip* you for whatever challenges you're facing. If you're constantly overwhelmed and stressed out, I want to help direct you toward positive living, even during tough situations. Challenges won't stop anytime soon. So, here's a set of tools to help you deal with real life challenges. These are the characteristics TOUGH people HAVE in common.

Watch your thoughts
For they become words.

Watch your words
For they become actions

Watch your actions
for they become habits.

Watch your habits
for they become character.

Watch your character
for it becomes your destiny.

Lao Tzu

TOUGH People
[THINK]
Adopting A Winning Mindset

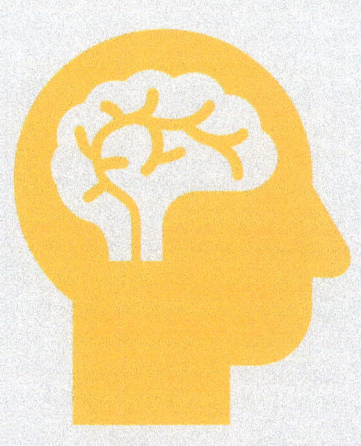

#2 TOUGH People [THINK] *Adopting A Winning Mindset*

To develop a TOUGH mentality, Habit #1 is all about adopting a winning mindset. Positive thinking helps us view storms in the proper perspective. Remember this:

Your current situation is not your final destination.

Tough times don't last.

It came to pass, it didn't come to stay.

Challenging times tend to overwhelm us when we *don't* keep them in context. *All it takes sometimes is seeing someone in a worse situation than you with a better attitude than you.*

Someone took that same situation you're complaining about and won with it.

[THINK] *Adopting A Winning Mindset*

Everything you see around you started as a single thought.

Buildings, tables, chairs, pots, T.V.s, smartphones, ALL started as a single thought. Could your environment be a result of negative thoughts?

TOUGH People understand the power of the mind in bringing about change in your life. The mind is fascinating. It's the most powerful supercomputer ever created.

Whatever you tell your mind, it will bend your reality towards that thought.

I know it sounds cliché, but you *have to*

speak victory into your life.

Walk by faith, not by sight.

I don't mean blind faith. This is a bold confidence in knowing this isn't your first rodeo. You've been here before. You've met challenges, faced giants, endured tough times before and come out on top! Like the old church song said, "I've seen too many victories to let defeat have the last word."

I wouldn't tell you this if I hadn't experienced for myself the power of a daily walk with God and a positive mindset *especially* in challenging situations.

Life is hard. Trust me, I get it. But I need to tell you that

you can get through it.

It's going to work out.

[THINK] *Adopting A Winning Mindset*

Almost 8 years ago now, one doctor who cared for our daughter described what life would be like **IF** we decided to save Kennedy versus "terminate care." He said it would be a crapshoot, her health was a roll of the dice. He said she would be "severely deformed" and "handicapped." He went on with the bad news, "It's gonna be a rollercoaster."

Rollercoasters are fun! We have had **a blast** raising Kennedy. Yes, it's been scary at times. Yes, it's been a bumpy ride. But that's why we love rollercoasters, right! We stand in line patiently for "it doesn't matter how long," *push past the fear and anxiety*, then buckle ourselves in and *enjoy the ride*. That's the mindset you have to take into your tough times. It takes some practice!

> "WE FIRST MAKE OUR HABITS, THEN OUR HABITS MAKE US."

TOUGH People
[TAP IN]

Detours and Distractions

#3 *TOUGH People [TAP In]* Detours and Distractions

> *"...A window shalt thou make to the ark, and in a cubit shalt thou finish it above."*
>
> *-Genesis 6:16*

If you've ever seen a cruise ship, you know they are huge! They're basically all-in-one hotel, amusement park, casino, restaurant, bar, gift shop, spa, nightclub, with 4 or 5 levels, upstairs, downstairs, indoor pool, outdoor pool...you get the idea. Now imagine one of those huge boats with just one small window. That brings us back to our 'cover story,' *Noah's Ark*.

> *Quick Summary:* **Anticipating the Great Flood, Noah constructed a massive ship that spanned 510 feet long, 85 feet wide, and 51 feet tall. That's about the length of 1 and a half football fields, the storage capacity of 450 standard semi-trailers, and a height greater than a 4-story house!**

Since we *don't* have details of what life was like for Noah on the ark during the storm, we'll look to the ship's design for insight. Noah built a **massive** ark *even by today's standards* but only left room for a very small opening (or window).

Why Are We Talking About Windows?

Literally speaking, windows control how much light, sound, and air pass through. They shape what we see, what we hear and what we feel. On a deeper level, Noah's single window calls our attention to maintaining our focus by controlling what we watch, what we listen to.

[TAP In] Detours and Distractions

Modern Windows

Technology has advanced quite a bit since Noah's days. Today, our digital "windows" play a big role in how we view ourselves and the world around us. They contribute to our daily mood and attitude.

Too Many Windows!

Today's windows are too many to count!

Instagram	smartphones	Hulu
Facebook	tablets	Netflix
Snapchat	computers	Roku
YouTube	T.V.s	Firestick
Tik Tok	laptops	Disney Plus

but wait, there's more

Zoom, Periscope, BET, CNN, NBC, MSNBC, Fox News, and the list goes on. The other day, I was on the computer doing some research on the internet. While I was working, I noticed even my windows had windows! I had 21 different tabs open on 2 separate browsers, with 3 to 4 ads per page, and 8 different computer programs running simultaneously.

We are bombarded day and night with data streams of

[dis]information

devastating world news

idle entertainment, and

images of people living the life we wish we had.

tough times don't last, **TOUGH PEOPLE DO**

[TAP In] *Detours and Distractions*

We have way TOO MANY WINDOWS dividing our attention and keeping us off track. No wonder we feel stressed! It's easy to overwhelm and confuse our systems when we get our news and our guidance from so many places at once *information overload!* And just like our computers and smartphones, we become sluggish, less efficient, and eventually shut down. Noah shows us that in his blueprint, tough times require laser-like focus.

KEEP THE MAIN THING THE MAIN THING

Here are some ways to TOUGH people narrow their focus.

● *Turn Off the News*

Of course, it is your civic duty to be informed about the world around you. Keep these things in mind on your quest for information.

A. *Most popular news coverage is highly subjective, riddled with opinions, and designed to play on your emotions.*

B. *Don't get trapped in the 24-hour news cycle.*

C. *Read*

D. *Find credible sources that provide clear objective viewpoints*

E. *Form your own opinions.*

F. *ALWAYS consider the source!*

● *Avoid the Rabbit Hole*

Let's face it, the internet is full of disinformation and deception. You can find information to support any outlandish claim if you look hard enough. We can easily get lost chasing bizarre conspiracy theories or trying to live up to social media personas.

● *Shrink Your Circle*

Tough times can be especially vulnerable, and you need the right people in your corner those who add value, bring encouragement and stability to your life. Don't share your business with everybody and only accept advice from those who have been where you want to go. It's important to keep a strong support system you can depend on

to be there for you

help keep you focused

and have necessary "tough" conversations.

Inconsistent "friends" are a problem all by themselves *they are not inner circle material.* Your inner circle is that small group of confidantes who have seen you at your worst, and still accept you for who you are. These are real friends who love you and push you to be your best. **Don't spend your time and energy on people who consistently let you down.** Focus on growing valuable relationships with people who accept you for **you** and *not* **what you have.**

WHEN SOMEONE SHOWS YOU THEIR TRUE COLORS, BELIEVE THEM.

tough times don't last, **TOUGH PEOPLE DO**

[TAP In] Detours and Distractions

● Cut Your Screen Time

Spending a few minutes watching YouTube, playing a game on your PS5, or connecting with friends on social media are all great ways to unwind and can escape from reality. However,

You can't escape the responsibility of tomorrow by avoiding it today.

– Abraham Lincoln

Limit Your Leisure

You may not have thought much about watching an episode or two (or 10!) of a new Netflix original series, or having a blast filling your camera roll with selfies as cute little creatures. But, if you're like me, there's been a time or two when you got a little carried away and spent way too much time on some something that didn't ADD value to your life. We live in a digital age. Spending time using media is inevitable and it's mostly harmless, but if you're unhappy with your current situation or *not* being all God created you to be, consider making a change to

spend more time and energy on productive activities that improve <u>you</u> and your situation.

TOUGH People Keep an [OPEN MIND]

Be a Solution

#4 TOUGH People [Keep an OPEN Mind] *Be a Solution*

TOUGH people keep their eyes open for **opportunity**. Keeping an open mind just means you *are* resourceful and constantly searching for answers

not dead set in your ways

not spending meaningless time desperate to get "back to normal."

Use creative problem solving to come up with new ideas and create innovative more efficient ways to complete everyday tasks. *So* many new businesses launch during times like these because there are a TON of problems *everywhere you look!*

More problems, more solutions

Solve A Problem
TOUGH People *find* a way to <u>be</u> a solution.

Try this approach to problem-solving.

Step 1: Identify the problem.

Step 2: Ask "why" until you get to the root cause of the problem.

Once you uncover the "real" problem you can identify a solution to fix it.

tough times don't last, **TOUGH PEOPLE DO**

[Keep an OPEN Mind] *Be a Solution*

Why? Why? Why? Why? Why?

I picked up the **5 WHY's** technique from my days managing customer service but you can repeat this process to get to the bottom of issues you come across. *Here's a simple example where* **a customer is unhappy**.

WHY *is the customer unhappy?*
The customer wants a discount.

WHY *does the customer want a discount?*
The customer waited longer than expected.

If you're following along, the next question would be
WHY *did the customer wait longer than expected?*

For the sake of time, I'll stop at 3 why's, but as you can see, we're already closer to the root of the problem. It's called **5 WHY's** *only* because you can usually find what is causing the issue with **5 WHY's** but keep digging until you get to the bottom of the problem.

 The answer is the first event in the chain of events that caused the frustration.

tough times don't last, **TOUGH PEOPLE DO** 28

[Keep an OPEN Mind] *Be a Solution*

This is **one** simple technique to becoming a problem-solver. Practice this exercise. Adapt it to fit your situation. The next time you encounter a problem, take some time getting down to the bottom of it and focus on fixing that! TOUGH people rely on creative problem-solving skills to

Develop Valuable Insight
Make Sound Decisions
and
Take Advantage of Opportunities.

Stay open to possibilities.

Always look to learn.

Avoid jumping to conclusions.

Don't rush to judgment.

[Keep an OPEN Mind] *Be a Solution*

Replace Dead End Language

Many of the 'default' words and phrases we use stop our minds from exploring and thinking things through. When we encounter roadblocks, we often reinforce our limits with our inner dialogue. These Conversation Killers bring finality to a thought or idea. When you experience a physical, mental, emotional, and even spiritual blocks, **keep the conversation going**. Allow your mind to reason with the objection and devise a way to overcome it.

TOUGH People stay open-minded by constantly asking questions and keeping the conversation going. Stay away from **limiting language**.

Ditch The 'I Don't Know's...Instead of saying "I don't know ___." say,

"I'll find out ___."

"I'll figure [it] out."

"Let me think about [it]."

Instead of focusing on limitations or reasons why you can't do something,

Ask yourself "How can I?" and you'll find a way.

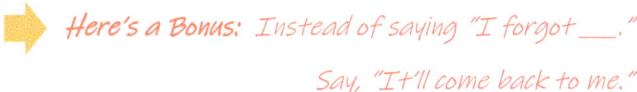 *Here's a Bonus: Instead of saying "I forgot ___."*

Say, "It'll come back to me."

tough times don't last, **TOUGH PEOPLE DO**

TOUGH People
Create
[OPPORTUNITY
Finding A Way

#5 TOUGH People [Create OPPORTUNITY] *Finding A Way*

This is the perfect sequel to "Keep an Open Mind." Unemployment skyrocketed thanks to coronavirus. With little to no help from the government, people have been forced to <u>pivot</u> and *discover new ways to make money.* One of the toughest challenges we face is experiencing financial problems. And with our country's current economic situation, this topic is as relevant as ever. This isn't an in-depth financial discussion *I'll leave that to The Finance Doctor (@drclemento).* We'll focus on discovering a few **Creative Money Finding Methods**. Why?

You may be unemployed.

Your hours have been cut.

You have a new, unexpected expense.

You're finally ready to step out on faith...

...execute your idea

...start your business.

[Create OPPORTUNITY] Finding A Way

You're saying to yourself
"I'm ready to OWN my business."
"I'm ready to fire my boss."   BUT   **"I NEED COINS!"**
I'm tired of building somebody else's dream."
"I'm ready to make my side hustle my main hustle."

You're not alone! One of the MAIN reasons people *don't* start a business is MONEY. This is a challenge, especially for people who have little to no disposable income or access to borrowing. Now, while you can get into business for next-to nothing or nothing *we'll discuss using OPM a little later*, I wanted to share some creative ways you can FIND money.

CMFM #1| Unclaimed Money

I made $20.80 in less than 5 minutes!

Each year, for various reasons, individuals AND organizations lose track of money or tangible property. That abandoned property or unclaimed money gets turned over to the office of unclaimed funds at your state's unclaimed property office. This office is in charge of finding the rightful owners and getting their money to them. Yet, hundreds of millions of dollars go unclaimed.

tough times don't last, **TOUGH PEOPLE DO**

[Create OPPORTUNITY] Finding A Way

Some common sources of unclaimed property are

dormant bank accounts
uncashed checks or money orders
rent or utility deposits
deposits, overpayments, & credit balances
HUD or FHA refunds

IRS refund checks
uncashed death benefits
life insurance proceeds
class action lawsuit settlements
and many more!

By law, the "holders" (banks, landlords, utility companies, etc.) of the assets turn this unclaimed money or property over to the government for safekeeping. While each state "tries" to locate the rightful owners, this money just sits in the state's Unclaimed Property Office until the rightful owner or heir claims it.

A man in Seattle, Washington found out he had over $9,000 in unclaimed money in the state's Unclaimed Property Office. The money was from a closed bank account of escrow money from a real estate transaction several years earlier. (Guess what) He had no idea it was there!

In Charleston, West Virginia over $480,000 was returned to a lost heir of a lady who had died several years earlier and didn't have a will or any known heirs. Her money was turned over to the state's unclaimed property office. The rightful heirs of a deceased person are entitled to unclaimed money being held by the State's Office. This money was just sitting in the state's unclaimed property offices.

tough times don't last, **TOUGH PEOPLE DO**

[Create OPPORTUNITY] Finding A Way

So, how do you know if you have Unclaimed Money? *It's easy.* Google "[Your state] unclaimed property." From there you should be able to find the website for your state treasurer.

- Search for funds, using your name or business name
- Select the property(ies) you wish to claim
- Complete the required claimant information

That's it! In under 5 minutes, I visited my state treasurer's website and claimed my money. Got my check within a week. Now you might be thinking, "all this over $20.80?!?"

"You didn't get $9,000."

"You didn't get half a million dollars."

Well, this isn't *really* about the amount. The money is negligible. What I'm hoping is to "teach you how to fish." I'm definitely not guaranteeing any amount. *However, if you DO by chance claim half a million dollars, my fee is 10%!*

[Create OPPORTUNITY] Finding A Way

This isn't really about the amount.
It IS about:

> YOU manifesting things into your life
>
> YOU getting active, going to GET your blessing
>
> YOU keeping an open mind and staying open to ideas
>
> YOU continuing to **A.S.K.**:
>> **Ask** "How CAN I _____?"
>>
>> **Seek** creative solutions by thinking outside the box.
>>
>> **Knock**. Don't wait for opportunity to come knocking

Create your opportunity.

Don't give up!

You're finding a way, finding solutions.

The difference between idea and reality is action!

Celebrate the wins!

That takes us right into Creative Money Finding Method #2.

tough times don't last, **TOUGH PEOPLE DO**

[Create OPPORTUNITY] Finding A Way

CMFM #2| Attracting Money

TOUGH People Create Opportunities through positive daily affirmations.

"I have the POWER to GET Wealth."

"Money comes to me easily, frequently, and abundantly!"

"Money comes to me easily, frequently, and abundantly!"

"Money comes to me easily, frequently, and abundantly!"

"Money comes to me easily, frequently, and abundantly!"

"Money comes to me easily, frequently, and abundantly!"

Write them down, repeat them over and over *and over again*. You'll start to experience the blessing, attract money, experience abundance, receive wisdom and million-dollar ideas, use Creative Money Finding Methods to find the resources and money you need.

Here are a few other Creative Money Finding Methods.

[Create OPPORTUNITY] *Finding A Way*

💡 CMFM| *Brainstorm*

If you're like facing a financial challenge, here's an exercise that will help you to begin manifesting the money you need. Let's say you need money for your mortgage, car note, startup money for your business, or a little extra cash flow. Every morning think of at least 20 ways you can get the money. Write them down.

Start with the amount you need or would like to make (for example, $1,000)

Then, list every way imaginable you could get $1,000. Write everything that comes to mind THE CRAZIER THE BETTER. So, your list may start something like this.

How to get this thousand dollar$

1. Rob a bank
2. Ask 1,000 people for $1 each
3. Ask 1 person for $1,000

Please do NOT rob a bank. You will go to jail...big people jail!

Not all your answers will be winners, but this exercise will get your wheels turning on finding your own Creative Money Finding Methods. It keeps you searching for solutions instead of settling on the problem. Sooner or later, you'll come across an answer that works for you! You *may* use just 1, a combination, or ALL the ideas you come up with.

I've kept you long enough. So, I'll try to breeze through the next few. Here are Creative Money Finding Methods 3-8.

[Create OPPORTUNITY] Finding A Way

CMFM #3| OPM (Other People's Money)

If you have an idea for a product or service, before getting in line for a bank loan. Create a mockup or prototype of your idea and launch it as a pre-order or presale. You can also use popular fundraising platforms like Kickstarter. This method also allows you to gain valuable market research.

CMFM #4| Shop Your House

Walk around your house and **shop**. Look for items people might buy. Simply take a picture, and list it on popular digital marketplaces where people are **looking** to buy.

Let Go	Etsy
Offer Up	Facebook Marketplace
eBay	

Then, sell them for a great price *all from your smartphone!*

CMFM #5| Survey Says

If you receive an envelope from 'Nielsen' you'll probably find 1 or 2 crisp dollar bills inside. They're yours to do with them whatever you please but if you complete and return the surveys, they will **pay you** to take them. Cash. They range in the amount but require very little time and effort.

[Create OPPORTUNITY] Finding A Way

CMFM #6| *Cut Your Cable*

How many cable TV channels do you *actually* watch? Break up with your cable company. You can opt into any of the popular streaming services for a fraction of the price. Michelle and I saved around $200 a month with one phone call.

CMFM #7| *Use Your Car*

If you're not familiar with Uber & Lyft they are the most popular ridesharing platforms. You get paid by helping people get where they need to go. If you already have a job or you're not much of a people person, you can find riders who share your commute and do just 1-2 trips a day. A trip before and after work can cover your gas to and from work. *These are 2 easy ways to turn a liability into an asset.*

CMFM #8| *Collaboration Over Competition*

Develop valuable partnerships to launch businesses, products, and services. *Don't let money be the reason you don't pursue your dreams.* Collaboration helps to eliminate many barriers to entry by working together to find creative solutions.

> **Step 1.** Bring something to the table by identifying your unique knowledge and/or skillset.
> **Step 2.** Find people whose resources *(time, talent, or treasure)* complement yours and vice versa.
> **Step 3.** Use your skills and talent as currency to create the opportunities you want to see. *Sometimes effort is your startup capital.*

tough times don't last, **TOUGH PEOPLE DO**

[Create OPPORTUNITY] Finding A Way

When it comes to *finding a way* out of tough situations, we tend to lean more towards competition *it's human nature!* But, **choosing** to compete usually means

 working to outshine the next person,

 creating opportunities to enrich ourselves *only*, or

 finding ways to satisfy our own selfish agenda *often at the expense of others*.

 Collaboration *on the other hand* brings out the *very* best in all of us; it draws on our greatest strengths. So, **identify**,

develop, and

leverage meaningful relationships with those whose knowledge and skillset are a great match!

Teamwork makes the dream work!

[Create OPPORTUNITY] Finding A Way

Shameless Plug!

I am collaborating with my *blood* brothers to develop a collection of resources that improve people's lives. We have worked together to develop a vision for their businesses & brands. We execute the vision by leveraging what each of us brings to the table *and everybody eats!*

(@drclemento) | www.4Qfinancial.com/store

(@captain006) | www.parent-child-connect.com

I bring _____ to the table:	**They** bring _____ to the table:
Creativity/ artistic eye	Industry experience/ expertise
Branding and graphic design experience	A growing platform
A knack for bringing ideas to life	

Q: *Do you constantly have great ideas but, lack the platform, knowledge, or experience in a particular industry?*

Answer: *Instead of competing with established individuals or brands (or ignoring the idea altogether), leverage your creativity to align with those who have more knowledge or experience in certain areas.*

Never let great ideas go to waste!

TOUGH People

[OWN IT]

Own Your I.P.

#6 TOUGH People [OWN IT] *Own Your I.P.*

Your Life Experience

Your intellectual property is your unique collection of knowledge, life experiences, and perspective of the world. It's based on your mind, your intellect. You've probably heard of the most common types:

copyrights, patents, trademarks, and trade secrets.

In short, *YOU are valuable!*

More and more, people are learning to build generational wealth by leveraging their intellectual property. Many entrepreneurs have pivoted to sharing their business knowledge and industry experience. Let's say you've worked 14 years in the same industry, or using certain software or equipment, you can package that experience in books and courses and sell it to consumers. Imagine the value you could add to somebody's life!

*People go in debt chasing
knowledge you already have*

Your life is a movie!

So, maybe you've experienced loss and depression

or you raised 6 black kids who all graduated college, you can tap into that experience to educate and touch somebody's life.

*YOU went through it...
OWN IT!*

TOUGH People

[UNDER-STAND]

Reflecting on the Past

#7 TOUGH People [UNDERSTAND] *Reflecting on the Past*

TOUGH people look to learn from every situation and gain wisdom from their experience.

> ## "…in all your getting, get understanding"
> – Proverbs 4:7

When we met, Michelle *that's Bae* introduced me to this symbol tattooed on her right shoulder. The Sankofa comes from Ghana. It means we *have to* continue moving forward while reflecting on our past. TOUGH people gain an appreciation for the strength it took to make it this far. When we look for understanding we can identify our strengths and ~~weaknesses~~ *growth opportunities*, where we perform well and where can stand to improve.

Appreciate who you are
…and what you're made of.

You'll realize your trials were necessary and what you learned you'll take to the next one.

TOUGH People
[GROW]
Uncomfortable Spaces

#8 *TOUGH People [GROW] Uncomfortable Spaces*

GET COMFORTABLE BEING UNCOMFORTABLE

TOUGH people look for opportunities to grow and challenge themselves. It's the same way athletes physically challenge their bodies to build their physique and stamina. We *have to* appreciate the value challenges bring, how they help us grow

>> take our lives to a new level

>> push us out of our comfort zones.

That's why I had to write this book! Juggling publishing a book while being a great husband, raising two beautiful children *1 with special needs*, figuring out a way to pay some bills, trying to remember to eat every day, cut the grass, paint the walls…isn't something I would necessarily recommend. *Responsibilities don't pause for you to write a book. And Life doesn't take a backseat to you pursuing your dreams. But,* ***if you can find it in yourself, to tough it out, I believe you will come out on top!***

[GROW] *Uncomfortable Spaces*

Set the date!

I knew this process would challenge me in ways I hadn't been challenged before. I knew it would push me to be great, make me uncomfortable. I knew I'd stress a little bit; I'd have to wrestle for clarity. I knew it would be hard and require some sacrifices. I knew I would have to labor with it. I knew it would not be easy. But I also knew it would turn around and help somebody keep going and come out on top!

*Challenge yourself,
As iron sharpens iron*

Challenge your strengths as well as your ~~weaknesses~~ growth opportunities.

tough times don't last, **TOUGH PEOPLE DO**

TOUGH People
[HELP]

Not in Vain

#9 TOUGH People [HELP] Not in Vain

I asked my dad one day what he wants his legacy to be. He said,

"If I can help one person as I go along, my living would not have been in vain."

TOUGH people **help** people. They realize giving is essential and find ways to serve. That's why Michelle and I started our non-profit organization, Kennedy's Courage, to inspire people by our journey and help families in situations like ours. Sharing details of our personal life isn't easy but helping somebody makes it all worth it.

That's also why the **Ogunyemi Family Foundation** established the Wisdom, Strength, and Endurance Scholarship to provide underrepresented minority students the opportunity to pursue higher education by eliminating financial barriers to students' success.

"GIVE TO LIVE AND LIVE TO GIVE"

- *Pastor Antoine Barriere*
Household of Faith Family Worship Church International

TOUGH People

Stay.

Think.

Tap in.

Keep an Open mind.

Create Opportunity.

Own it!

Understand.

Grow.

Help.

Are you **TOUGH**?

www.ingramcontent.com/pod-product-compliance
Lightning Source LLC
Chambersburg PA
CBHW040107120526
44589CB00039B/2796